101854

Vibrations

by Lola M. Schaefer

Consulting Editor: Gail Saunders-Smith, Ph.D.

Consultant: P. W. Hammer, Ph.D., Acting Manager of Education, American Institute of Physics

Pebble Books

an imprint of Capstone Press
Mankato, Minnesota

Pebble Books are published by Capstone Press
818 North Willow Street, Mankato, Minnesota 56001
http://www.capstone-press.com

Library of Congress Cataloging-in-Publication Data
Schaefer, Lola M., 1950–
    Vibrations/by Lola M. Schaefer.
    p. cm.—(The way things move)
    Includes bibliographical references and index.
    Summary: Simple text and photographs show different objects that vibrate.
    ISBN 0-7368-0399-8
    1. Vibration—Juvenile literature. 2. Sound—Juvenile literature [1. Vibration.
2. Sound.] I. Title. II. Series.
QC241.S32   2000
531'.32—dc21   99-19422
                                                                          CIP

Note to Parents and Teachers

The series The Way Things Move supports national science standards for units on understanding motion and the principles that explain it. The series also shows that things move in many different ways. This book describes and illustrates vibrations. The photographs support early readers in understanding the text. The repetition of words and phrases helps early readers learn new words. This book also introduces early readers to subject-specific vocabulary words, which are defined in the Words to Know section. Early readers may need assistance to read some words and to use the Table of Contents, Words to Know, Read More, Internet Sites, and Index/Word List sections of the book.

Table of Contents

4

Vibrations are fast movements back and forth.

Vibrations in air
make sounds.

Hummingbird wings vibrate.

Drums vibrate.

Guitar strings vibrate.

Vocal cords vibrate.

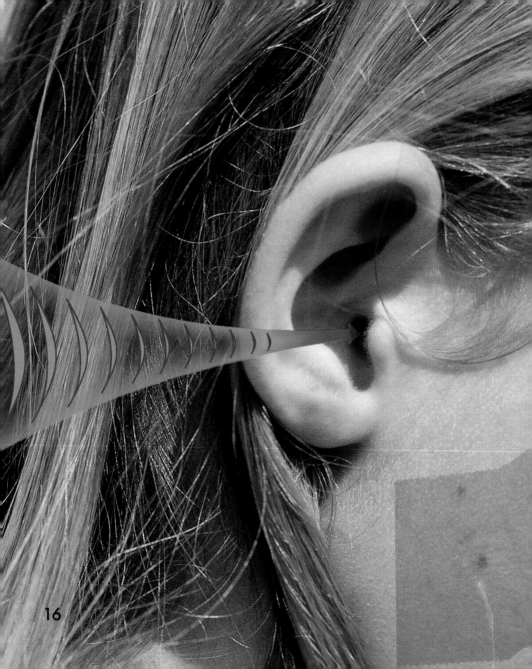

Your ears collect vibrations.

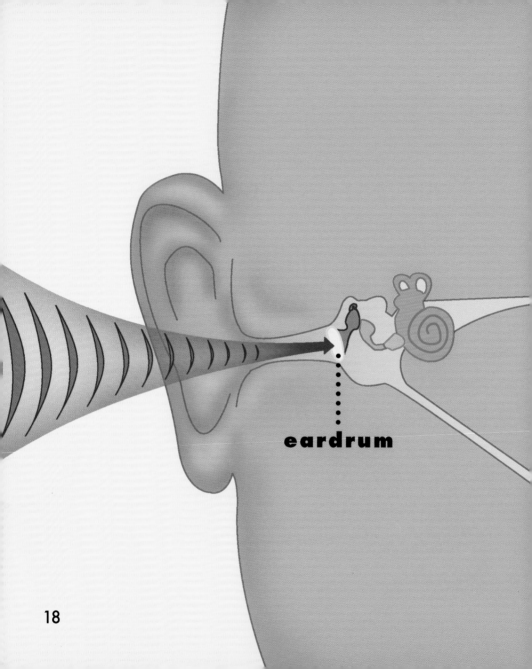

eardrum

Then your eardrum vibrates.

The vibrations become
the sounds you hear.

Words to Know

collect—to gather something; the outer ear collects vibrations and sends them to the eardrum.

eardrum—a thin skin inside the ear; the eardrum vibrates when sound waves hit it.

guitar—a musical instrument with strings that can be plucked or strummed; each string on the guitar makes a different sound.

hear—to sense sounds through your ears; ears change vibrations into sounds.

hummingbird—a small bird; hummingbird wings make a humming sound when hummingbirds fly.

movement—the act of changing position from place to place

sound—something that is heard; sounds move through the air as sound waves.

vocal cords—bands of skin in a person's air pipe; air from the lungs passes through the vocal cords; this causes the vocal cords to vibrate and make sound.

Read More

Frost, Helen. *Hearing.* The Senses. Mankato, Minn.: Pebble Books, 2000.

Pinna, Simon de. *Sound.* Science Projects. Austin, Texas: Raintree Steck-Vaughn, 1998.

Robinson, Fay. *Sound All Around.* Rookie Read-about Science. Chicago: Children's Press, 1994.

Internet Sites

Making a Shoe Box Guitar
http://www.eecs.umich.edu/mathscience/
funexperiments/agesubject/lessons/guitar.html

The Soundry: The Physics of Sound
http://library.advanced.org/19537/Physics.html

Sounds Like Science: Drums
http://www.eecs.umich.edu/mathscience/
funexperiments/agesubject/lessons/other/una4.html

The Straw Flute
http://129.82.166.181/Straw.html

Index/Word List

air, 7
back, 5
collect, 17
drums, 11
eardrum, 19
ears, 17
fast, 5
forth, 5
guitar, 13
hear, 21

hummingbird, 9
movements, 5
sounds, 7, 21
strings, 13
vibrate, 9, 11, 13,
   15, 19
vibrations, 5, 7,
   17, 21
vocal cords, 15
wings, 9

Word Count: 38
Early-Intervention Level: 9

Editorial Credits
Martha E. H. Rustad, editor; Timothy Halldin, cover designer; Kevin T. Kes and
   Linda Clavel, illustrators; Heidi Schoof, photo researcher

Photo Credits
Bill Losh/FPG International LLC, 20
FPG International LLC, 12
Index Stock Imagery, cover, 4
Photo Network/Nancy Hoyt Beicher, 10
Unicorn Stock Photos/Ron P. Jaffe, 6
Visuals Unlimited/Joe McDonald, 8; Jeff Greenberg, 14; Bernd Wittich, 16
West Stock, 1